2/05

PUBLIC LIBRARY DISTRICT
W9-CCN-009
3 2186 00145

Light

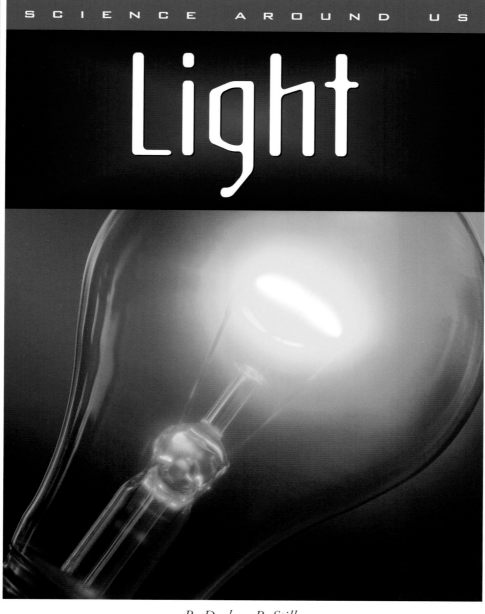

By Darlene R. Stille

THE CHILD'S WORLD®
CHANHASSEN, MINNESOTA

Fossil Ridge Public Library District
Braidwood, IL 60408

The Child's World

Published in the United States of America by The Child's World®
PO Box 326, Chanhassen, MN 55317-0326
800-599-READ
www.childsworld.com

Content Adviser:
Mats Selen, PhD,
Professor of Physics,
University of Illinois,
Urbana, Illinois

Photo Credits: Cover: Randy Faris/Corbis. Interior: Bettmann/Corbis: 12, 30-top, 30-bottom; Corbis: 6 (Firefly Productions) , 10, 11 (A. & J. Verkaik) , 15 (Ariel Skelley) , 27 (Reuters NewMedia Inc.) , 30-middle (Hulton-Deutsch Collection); Custom Medical Stock Photo: 17; Getty Images: 16 (Taxi/Kate Powers) , 28 (Digital Vision); Getty Images/ The Image Bank: 19 (D2 Productions) , 26 (Steve Dunwell); Getty Images/Stone: 20 (Angela Wyant) , 25 (Phil Degginger); Photo Researchers: 4 (Joseph Nettis) , 9 (E. R. Degginger) , 13 (Alfred Pasieka) , 18 (David R. Frazier); PictureQuest: 5 (David Job/ Alaska Stock Images) , 7 (Frank Kletschkus/ImageState-Pictor) , 21 (Norbert Wu/Norbert Wu Productions) , 22 (Creatas) , 23 (Ted Dayton/Index Stock Imagery) .

The Child's World®: Mary Berendes, Publishing Director

Editorial Directions, Inc.: E. Russell Primm, Editorial Director; Pam Rosenberg, Line Editor; Katie Marsico, Assistant Editor; Matt Messbarger, Editorial Assistant; Susan Hindman, Copy Editor; Susan Ashley, Proofreader; Peter Garnham, Olivia Nellums, and Katherine Trickle, Fact Checkers; Tim Griffin/IndexServ, Indexer; Cian Laughlin O'Day, Photo Researcher; Linda S. Koutris, Photo Selector

The Design Lab: Kathleen Petelinsek, Design; Kari Thornborough, Page Production

Copyright © 2005 by The Child's World®
All rights reserved. No part of this book may be reproduced or utilized in any form or by any means without written permission from the publisher.

Library of Congress Cataloging-in-Publication Data
Stille, Darlene R.
  Light / by Darlene R. Stille.
    v. cm. — (Science around us)
Contents: Discovering light—Where light comes from—The colors of light—Light bounces and bends—Hot and cool light—Using light.
  ISBN 1-59296-221-1 (lib. bdg. : alk. paper) 1. Light—Juvenile literature. [1. Light.] I. Title. II. Science around us (Child's World (Firm))
  QC360.S78 2005
  535—dc22
                                              2003027225

TABLE OF CONTENTS

CHAPTER ONE

DISCOVERING LIGHT

The first people on Earth knew they could see when it was light outside. At night, they could not see. They got up in the morning when sunlight made the world bright. They could see their friends and family during daylight. They could hunt animals. They could gather fruits and nuts.

Without sunlight, they could not see where they were walking or do any work. So, after the sun set, they wrapped up in animal skins and furs and went to sleep.

When the sun set, prehistoric people went to sleep. They had no way to light up the darkness.

Fire was one of the first forms of light that allowed people to see in the darkness.

Eventually, people learned to make light, which they could use after it got dark outside. First, they used fire to help them see. A circle of light from a glowing campfire let them see one another. The light given off by burning torches helped them see where they were walking at night.

Electricity provides us with a source of energy to power lights, computers, and many other things that we use every day.

Later, people learned to make candles and oil lamps, whose light could be used for reading.

Today, **electricity** provides light after the sun sets. You flick a switch on the wall of your room, and an electric light comes on. Electric light makes your room bright. You don't have to go to bed as soon as it gets dark outside. You can stay up to read, play games, or do homework.

Light does a lot more than allow us to see. Sunlight makes Earth warm enough for life. Light from the Sun makes plants grow. The growing plants give off the oxygen people need to breathe. We use plants for food as well. We can also burn coal and oil, which are formed from plants that died long ago.

Scientists learned that light is a kind of **energy.** They call the energy of light radiant energy. Visible light is the kind of radiant energy that we can see. There are other kinds of light that we can't see. We can't see rays of **infrared** or **ultraviolet** light.

These ferns, like all plants, require light from the sun to help them grow.

CHAPTER TWO

WHERE LIGHT COMES FROM

Light is called natural or artificial, depending on where it comes from. Natural light comes from the Sun and other stars, which shine and give off light. Some animals, such as fireflies, can make their own natural light.

Artificial light comes from things that people make. The flame of a candle gives off light. Electricity makes glass lightbulbs glow and give off light. Batteries power the artificial light of a flashlight.

Many things give off light when they get hot. An iron bar glows when it is heated in a furnace. Deep inside Earth, hot, melted rock glows. This rock looks like a river of fire when it gushes out of a volcano. The metal wires inside a toaster glow when they heat up to toast a piece of bread.

Both natural and artificial light come from atoms. Atoms are tiny pieces of matter much too small for you to see. Electrons are even tinier parts of atoms. Sometimes changes inside an atom give off light. Sometimes the wiggling of electrons gives off light.

Molten lava is so hot that it gives off light as it flows out of a volcano.

You can think of the way that light travels in two ways. One way is to picture light traveling as little bundles of energy. These bundles are called photons. One photon is so tiny that you would never be able to see just one.

You can also picture light traveling as a wave. Light waves are different from other kinds of waves. For example, you can see waves ripple across water and go up and down. Water, sound, and other waves must travel through something. Only light waves can travel through empty space.

Nothing can travel faster than light. Light travels through space at about 299,792 kilometers (186,282 miles) per second.

A flash of light could go around Earth's equator about seven and a half times in one second.

Astronomers use the speed of light to measure long distances in space. They measure distance in light-years. One light-year is the distance that a flash of light travels in one year, about 9.46 trillion kilometers (5.88 trillion miles). The next closest star beyond our Sun is about 4.3 light-years away. That means it would take a spaceship traveling at the speed of light 4.3 years to reach that star. The Milky Way, the galaxy our Sun is in, is about 100,000 light-years wide. So it would take a spaceship traveling at the speed of light 100,000 years to cross the Milky Way.

CHAPTER THREE

THE COLORS
OF LIGHT

The visible light that you can see is made of every color of the
rainbow. Visible light is also called white light. White light is
made of red, orange, yellow, green, blue, indigo, and violet light.

Visible light is made up of every color in this rainbow.

Born in 1642, English scientist and mathematician Sir Isaac Newton performed experiments with light. He was the first person to discover that white light is really made up of many different colors.

Sir Isaac Newton, an English scientist, discovered that white light is made up of all these colors. He let a beam of sunlight shine through a piece of glass with many sides, called a prism. Newton's prism broke the white light into those different colors.

You can think of light rays as being like strands of color. Each color of the rainbow blends into the color next to it. The colors between violet (on one end of the rainbow) and red (on the other end) make up visible white light, the light you can see. Beyond the violet light is ultraviolet light that you cannot see. Ultraviolet rays can cause sunburn. Beyond the red light is infrared light. You cannot see infrared rays, but you can feel them as heat.

Newton made important discoveries about optics. Optics is the study of light—what it is, how it behaves, and how we can use it.

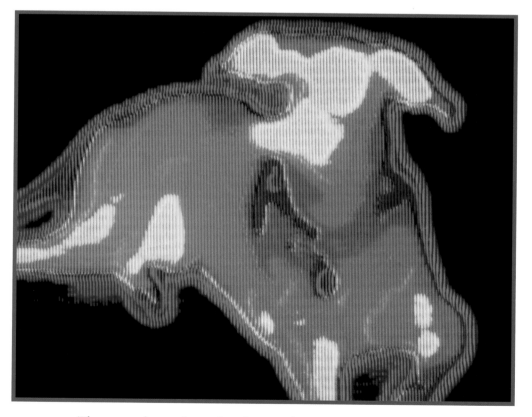

Thermography can be used to detect and measure the heat, or infrared radiation, given off by different areas of a body. If you look carefully, you can see that this is a thermographic image of a dog.

CHAPTER FOUR

LIGHT BOUNCES AND BENDS

Light can travel in a straight line or it can bounce and bend. It travels in a straight line until it hits something. What happens then depends upon what it hits.

Some things that light hits are **transparent.** Clear window glass is transparent, so sunlight goes right through it and you can also see through it. Some things that light hits are opaque. If something is opaque, light rays cannot go through it and you cannot see through it. A brick wall is opaque. Light rays bounce off the surface of a brick wall. They bounce off of anything that you cannot see through. This bouncing is called reflection. Reflection lets you see things. You can see a brick wall, cars, books, and your friends because light bounces off of these things.

Light rays bounce every which way when they hit bumpy opaque surfaces. That is why you can see your friend's face. Light rays bounce in a very orderly way when they hit a smooth, opaque surface. That is why you can see a reflection of your face in a mirror or a piece of shiny metal.

Opaque materials also "soak up" colors that make up light. When

Light rays bouncing off of a mirror let you see your reflection.

sunlight hits a red dress, the dress soaks up all the colors in the

sunlight except red, which bounces off the dress so you can see it.

This is why different things are different colors.

When light rays hit something that is red, the red object soaks up all of the colors of light except for red. The red light bounces off of the object so you can see it.

Light travels faster through some materials than others. Light rays go faster through air than through water. Light bends when it speeds up or slows down. You can see what happens when light speeding through air hits water. It slows down. Put a pencil in a glass of water. The pencil looks like it is broken in two at the surface of the water. The pencil looks broken because light rays bend. The bending of light is called refraction.

Light slows down when it hits the water in this glass. This causes it to bend, making the pencil appear broken.

WHY THE SKY IS BLUE

The sky is not really blue. It just looks blue. The sky looks blue because of the way that sunlight acts or behaves.

Sunlight is made up of all the colors of the rainbow— red, orange, yellow, green, blue, indigo, and violet. All the colors travel together until the sunlight gets to Earth's atmosphere. Above Earth's atmosphere, the Sun looks bright but the sky looks black. Inside the atmosphere, the sunlight bumps into tiny bits, or particles, of gas, dust, raindrops, snowflakes, and ice.

When sunlight bumps into a particle, the colors in the light bounce around. This bouncing around is called scattering. The different rays of colored light scatter, or go off, in new directions.

Blue light scatters more than any other color of light. Blue light gets scattered all over the sky and makes the sky look blue. The sky looks red when the Sun sets. Red and orange light scatter less than any other colors. The sunset looks red or orange because light from the Sun has to go through more atmosphere than it does when the Sun is overhead. The other colors get scattered away, leaving red and orange to bring you beautiful sunsets.

CHAPTER FIVE

HOT AND COOL LIGHT

T hings that are really hot give off light. Some things that are cool can also give off light. Light can be either hot or cool. Light that comes from hot things is called incandescent light. Light that comes from cool things is called luminescent light.

The Sun is blazing hot. The light that comes from the Sun is incandescent light. An ordinary lightbulb gets very hot. The light that comes from it is

Lightbulbs give off incandescent light.

incandescent light. Never touch a lightbulb that is on, because it could burn you.

A fluorescent (fluh-RESS-uhnt) lamp feels much cooler than a lightbulb. Chemicals in a fluorescent lamp give off light when electricity goes through the tube. Fluorescent light is cool light, or luminescent light. You can touch a fluorescent lamp without getting burned.

The bodies of some animals have chemicals that give off luminescent light. The bright flash of a firefly at night comes from luminescent light.

Fluorescent lamps, such as those in this ceiling fixture, give off luminescent light.

The glow from small lantern fish that live in the ocean is luminescent light.

Scientists call the cool light that comes from animals bioluminescence (bye-oh-loo-muh-NES-ents). Some animals use their cool light to find mates. Other animals use their cool light to attract smaller animals that they catch and eat.

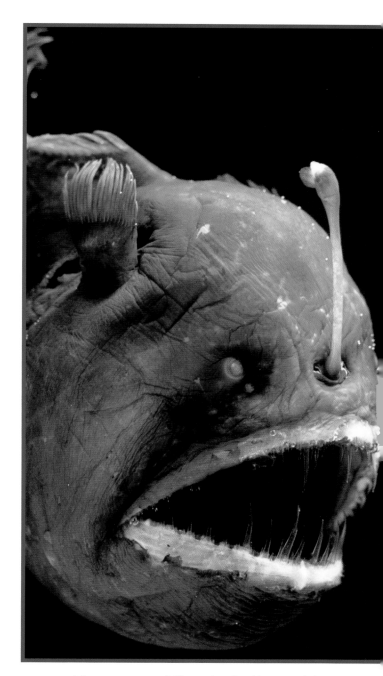

There are many different kinds of lantern fish. Lantern fish use their bioluminescence to attract mates, defend themselves, or to lure prey.

CHAPTER SIX

USING LIGHT

You use light for many things besides seeing. You can use strong light to get warm. Standing in sunlight makes you feel warmer than standing in the shade. A heat lamp in your bathroom has a powerful light that gives off lots of heat. It can warm you when you take a shower or bath.

Electric eyes are like switches that turn things on and off. Light and electricity make them work. Electric eyes can turn streetlights on

You can use the strong light of the sun to warm up after a swim in cool water.

when it gets dark and can

turn them off after the

sun rises. Your

garage door may

have an electric

eye that keeps it

from accidentally

closing on you or

your pet. Electric

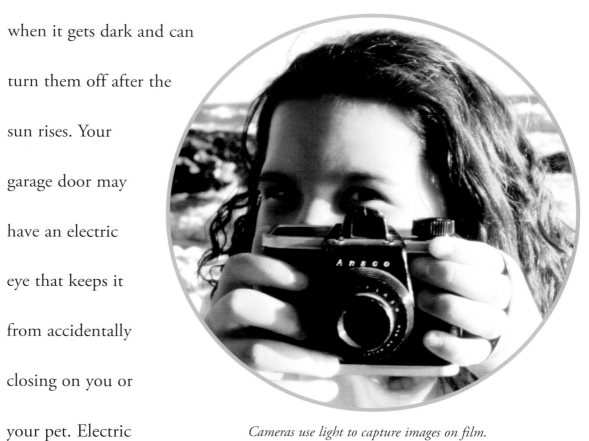

Cameras use light to capture images on film.

eyes in factories can count bottles, toys, or boxes of cereal passing by.

Cameras use light to make pictures. You need light to take snapshots or make movies. Your television set needs light to bring you your favorite shows. A television camera uses light to make pictures. Your television screen lights up to show you the pictures.

A special kind of light called laser light can do even greater things. A laser gives off thin beams of very powerful light. The heat from powerful laser light can cut through steel. Doctors use less-powerful lasers to do operations. CD and DVD players use beams of laser light to play music or show movies. Laser beams in a grocery store scan price codes printed on cans, boxes, and bottles. Lasers can make 3-D pictures called holograms.

Laser light even allows you to talk to your friends on the telephone. Your voice gets changed into a kind of code. A laser flashes the code through thin strands of glass called optical fibers. These fibers can be thinner than one of your hairs.

Optical fibers can also carry TV programs and let you use your computer to surf the Internet. One thin optical fiber can carry more signals than thousands of ordinary telephone wires.

Grocery stores use laser beams to scan price codes on items and make the cashier's job easier.

Doctors use optical fibers and tiny TV cameras to see inside the body.

There is more to light than meets the eye. Scientists and engineers are finding new uses for light all the time.

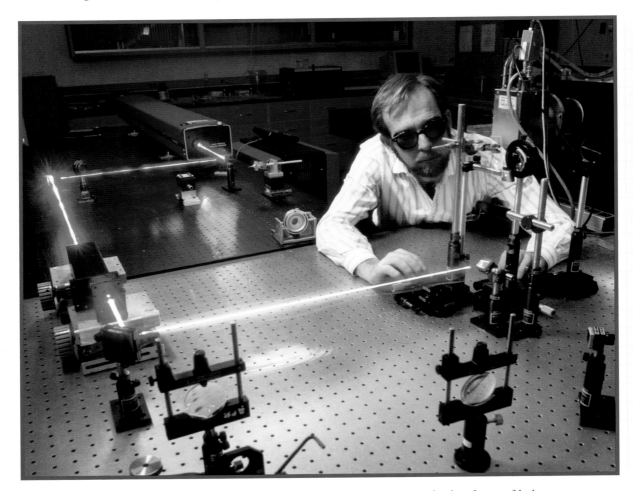

Scientists and engineers continue to experiment with lasers and other forms of light.
They hope to find even more uses for this important form of energy.

"SEEING" WITH OTHER KINDS OF RAYS

There are many kinds of rays other than visible light rays. Light is just one kind of radiant energy. Scientists use other kinds of light rays to "see" what is going on in our world and our universe. They sometimes use special machines that can see these invisible rays.

X-ray machines use X-rays to see inside the body. An X-ray can go through your skin and muscles easily, but is usually stopped by your bones. An X-ray picture can help a doctor tell if a bone is broken. Dentists use X-rays to look inside teeth. X-rays can tell if there is any tooth decay.

Some night vision cameras and goggles use infrared rays to see in the dark. Infrared rays come from heat in bodies and other things. Soldiers, police officers, and hunters can see at night with night vision goggles.

Special telescopes look for X-rays, ultraviolet rays, and gamma rays coming from deep space. X-ray telescopes help astronomers study the centers of galaxies, hot gases between galaxies, and black holes. Astronomers use ultraviolet telescopes to learn how stars form and what clouds of gas between stars are made of. They use gamma ray telescopes to study strange deep-space objects called pulsars and quasars.

GLOSSARY

astronomers (uh-STRON-uh-merz) Astronomers are scientists who study the stars, planets, and outer space.

electricity (i-lek-TRISS-uh-tee) Electricity is a form of energy that is caused by the motion of small particles in atoms called electrons.

energy (EN-ur-jee) Energy is the ability to do work.

infrared (in-fra-RED) Something that is infrared is outside the range of visible light, beyond the color red.

transparent (transs-PAIR-uhnt) If something is clear and lets light go through it, it is said to be transparent.

ultraviolet (uhl-truh-VYE-uh-lit) Light that is outside the range of visible light, beyond the color violet, is said to be ultraviolet.

X-ray (EKS-ray) An X-ray is an invisible ray of high-energy light that can pass through some things that are solid.

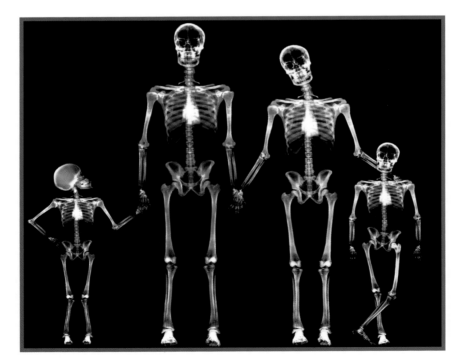

X-rays let us see inside the human body and take pictures of the human skeleton.

DID YOU KNOW?

▶ Ultraviolet light can be very dangerous. Rays of ultraviolet light can tan your skin, but they can also give you a sunburn. Ultraviolet light can even cause skin cancer. Covering up with hats and clothes or putting on sunscreen can help block out ultraviolet rays.

▶ Translucent materials let some light go through them. You can see blurred shapes through translucent glass or plastic. Translucent glass may be frosted or have a rough surface that some light rays bounce off of.

▶ Glowworms, the young larvae of insects such as fireflies, give off cool bioluminescent light. Millions of glowworms hang from the ceilings and walls of the Waitomo Glowworm Caves in New Zealand. People take boat rides through the caves to see the light given off by the glowworms.

▶ One-celled sea creatures called dinoflagellates give off cool bioluminescent light. Their light gives a glow at night to waves that come from ships and even dolphins swimming by.

▶ Bending light rays cause jewelry made with diamonds and other gems to sparkle. Light bends when it goes from air into gems.

▶ Did you ever drive down a road and see a pool of water in the distance? Then when you got there, the pool of water had disappeared? You saw a mirage. Bending light rays make mirages. Light rays bend when they go through air that has different temperatures. Sunlight makes air just above the ground warmer than air higher up. Sunlight bends upward when it hits the warmer air. The bending light makes a mirage that looks like water.

▶ Light beams from lasers can help guide ships, airplanes, and missiles. Laser beams can guide construction workers trying to line up the walls and ceilings of a building.

▶ Astronomers study the colors of light coming from distant stars to learn what the stars are made of and how far away the stars are. The color of the light can also help scientists figure out how fast the stars are moving.

TIMELINE

130 B.C.   Ptolemy calculates angles of refraction for light passing through different things.

A.D. 1604   Johannes Kepler (top left) describes how the eye focuses light.

1637   René Descartes figures out the angles at which rainbows can be seen, depending on the Sun's position in the sky.

1673   Ignace Pardies comes up with his wave explanation of the refraction of light.

1675   Isaac Newton proposes his theory of light.

1676   Olaus Roemer announces his measurement of the speed of light.

1690   Christian Huygens publishes his *Treatise on Light*.

1704   Isaac Newton publishes *Opticks*.

1728   Astronomer James Bradley (right) determines the speed of light based on his study of starlight.

1800   Infrared radiation from the Sun is discovered by William Herschel.

1801   Scientist Johann Ritter discovers ultraviolet radiation.

1849   French physicists Armand Fizeau and Jean-Bernard Foucault come up with the first accurate measurement of the speed of light by conducting experiments not related to the study of astronomy.

1871   English scientist Lord Rayleigh explains that the sky is blue and sunsets are red and orange because of the scattering of light as it hits particles in Earth's atmosphere.

1873   Scottish physicist James Clerk Maxwell describes light as one form of electromagnetic radiation.

1901   German physicist Wilhelm Conrad Röntgen (bottom left) receives the Nobel Prize for Physics for his discovery of X-rays.

HOW TO LEARN MORE ABOUT LIGHT

At the Library

Cooper, Christopher. *Light: From Sun to Bulbs.*
Chicago: Heinemann Library, 2003.

Richards, Jon, Ian Moores, and Ian Thompson (illustrators). *Light and Sight.*
Brookfield, Conn.: Copper Beech Books, 1999.

Tocci, Salvatore. *Experiments with Light.*
New York: Children's Press, 2001.

On the Web

VISIT OUR HOME PAGE FOR LOTS OF LINKS ABOUT LIGHT:
http://www.childsworld.com/links.html
Note to Parents, Teachers, and Librarians: We routinely verify our Web links to make sure they're safe, active sites—so encourage your readers to check them out!

Places to Visit or Contact

MUSEUM OF SCIENCE AND INDUSTRY
To see the IMAGING: Tools of Science exhibit and learn more about what scientists have learned about light and how it can be used in different fields
57th Street and Lake Shore Drive
Chicago, IL 60637
773/684-1414

SCIENCE MUSEUM OF VIRGINIA
To see the Light and Vision exhibit
2500 West Broad Street
Richmond, VA 23220
800/659-1727

INDEX

3 2186 00145 3041

About the Author

Darlene R. Stille is a science writer. She has lived in Chicago, Illinois, all her life. When she was in high school, she fell in love with science. While attending the University of Illinois she discovered that she also loved writing. She was fortunate to find a career that allowed her to combine both her interests. Darlene Stille has written more than 60 books for young people.

Fossil Ridge Public Library District
Braidwood, IL 60408